D is for Detroit's ABC's

Written by
Elizabeth Yohannes

To the very best part of me, London and Lennox, you insprire me daily and I love you more than words could ever convey. May the beautiful memories of our countless adventures always remain in your minds and hearts.

Dear Reader Friend,

We are so excited for you to journey with us on this fun learning adventure. Let's go!

Love,

London & Lennox

SCAN FOR ANIMATED VIDEO

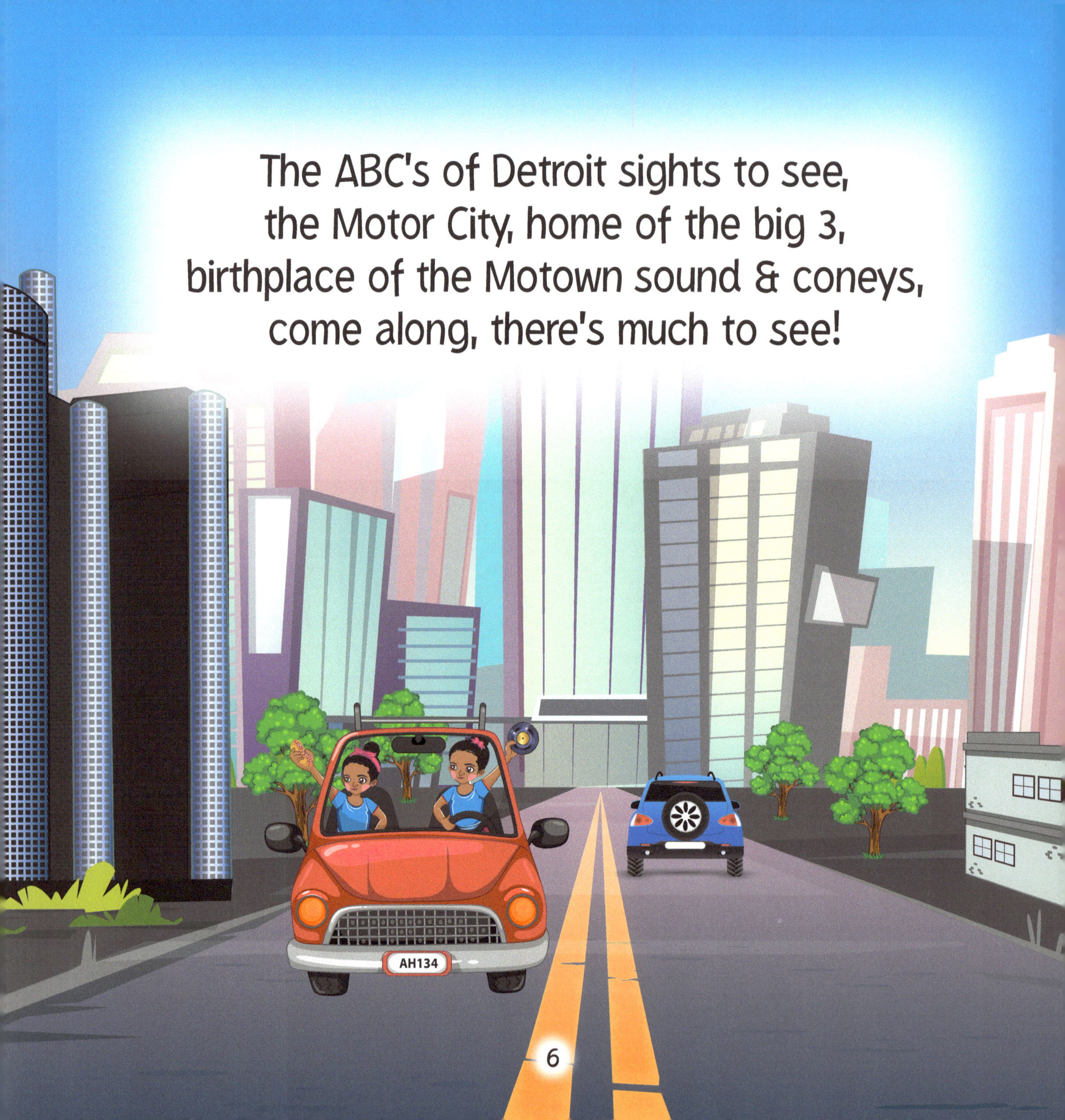
The ABC's of Detroit sights to see,
the Motor City, home of the big 3,
birthplace of the Motown sound & coneys,
come along, there's much to see!

Aa

A is for **A**mbassador Bridge,
allowing Detroit, Michigan to Canada passage.

Bb

B is for Belle Isle,
with the USA's only marble lighthouse.

Cc

C is for Campus Martius, summer beach
and winter ice skating fun for us.

Dd

D is for Detroit Historical Museum,
with many city exhibits for you to take in.

E e

E is for Eastern Market,
where vendors bring goods, have your pick.

Ff
F is for Fisher Building,
called the largest art object in the D.
FISHER THEATRE
12

Gg

G is for Greenfield Village,
nearly 100 buildings in history for you to visit.

Hh

H is for Henry Ford Museum,
largest U.S. indoor-outdoor one you can be in.

Ii

I is for Institute,
Detroit Institute of Arts, many works to peruse.

Jj
J is for Joe Louis Monument,
a tribute to the boxer known as The Fist.
16

Kk
K like in Beacon Park,
summer fun or cool lights in winter
after dark.

Little Caesars
Arena
Ll
L is for Little Caesars Arena,
see more sports teams and shows
than you can dream of.
18

Mm

M is for Michigan Science Center,
for kids and all ages, inspiring inventors.

Nn

N is for Nature Center on Belle Isle,
come see Michigan's wildlife, so versatile.

Oo

O is for Opera House,
where the Michigan Opera Theatre
attracts quite a crowd.

Pp

P is for People Mover,
riding 'round movers, shakers and the doers.

Qq

Q is for QLINE,
a streetcar on Woodward that you can ride.

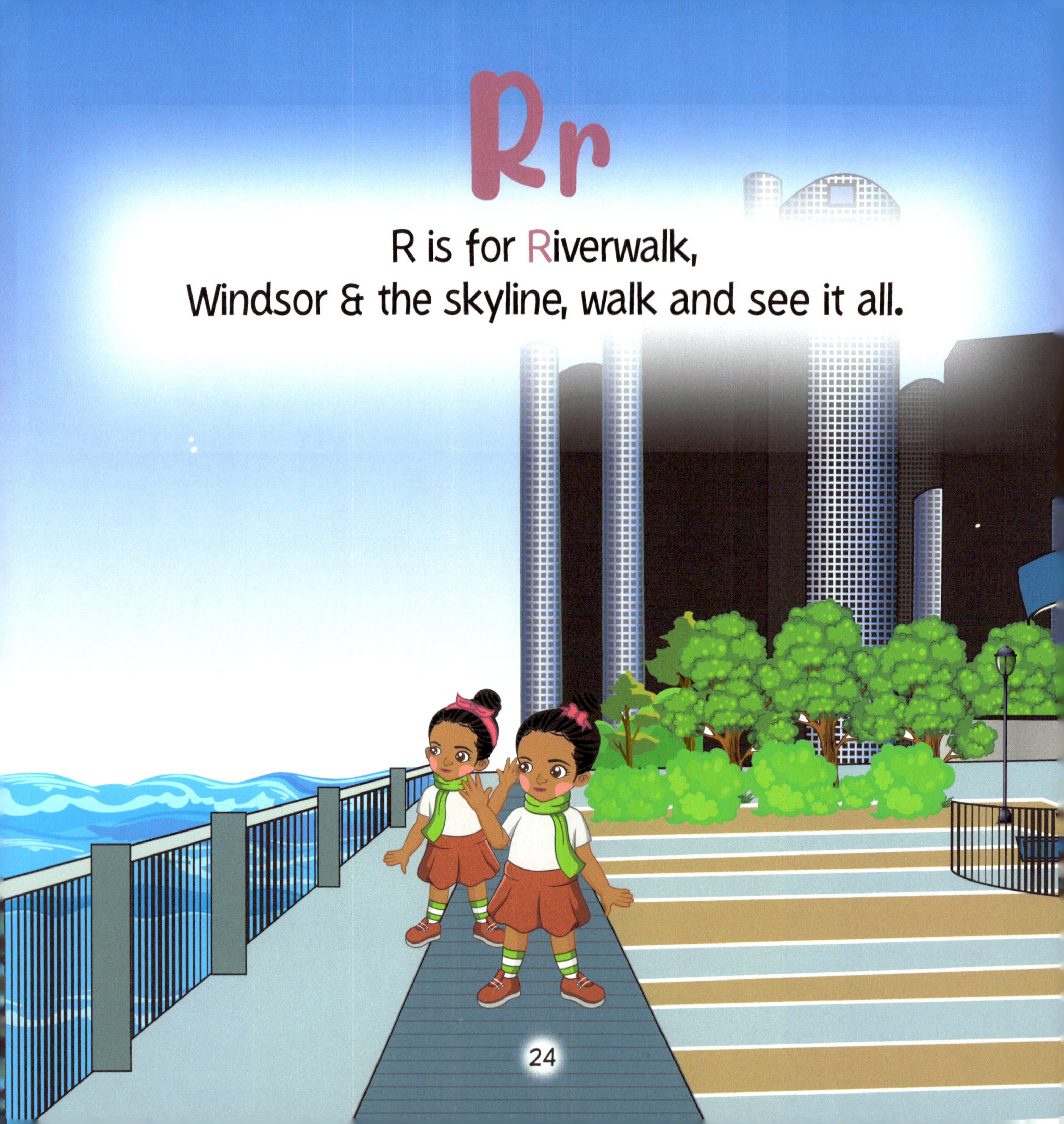

Rr
R is for Riverwalk,
Windsor & the skyline, walk and see it all.
24

S s
S is for Spirit of Detroit,
progress and hope, is what it's meant to voice.

T t

T like in Detroit-Windsor Tunnel,
world's only underwater one for cars
that's international.

Uu

U like in Hitsville U.S.A.
home of the Motown sound, from back in the day.

27

Vv

V like in Lexus Velodrome,
with an indoor track cyclists can call their home.

Ww

W is for Warren Avenue,
where the African-American history
museum can be viewed.

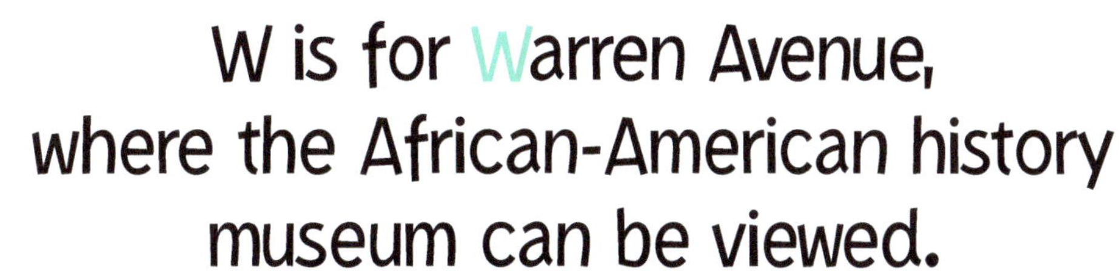

X like in Detroit's Fox Theatre,
the first ever to have escalators and elevators.
FOX

Yy
Y like in Michigan Labor Legacy
Monument that honors union workers' history.

Zz

Z like in Detroit Zoo,
first in the US to have bars on habitats removed.

The ABC's of Detroit sights to see, the Motor City, home of the big 3, birthplace of the Motown sound & coneys, you should come and visit our great city!

CONVERSATION STARTERS

Read the questions below and answer them.

1. What kind of animals do you think you would find at The Detroit Zoo?

2. What are some ways you can get to Canada from Detroit?

3. What types of goods do you think are sold at Eastern Market?

4. What kind of activities can you do at Campus Martius?

5. What types of sports are played at Little Caesars Arena?

DETROIT BUCKET LIST

Make a list of things you'd like to do when you get the opportunity to explore Detroit. Be sure to check off each box after you've done each.

1. _______________________________ ☐

2. _______________________________ ☐

3. _______________________________ ☐

4. _______________________________ ☐

5. _______________________________ ☐

6. _______________________________ ☐

7. _______________________________ ☐

THE END